AF575594

GUIDEBOOKS FOR THE DEAD

Also by Cynthia Cruz

Dregs (2018)
How the End Begins (2016)
Wunderkammer (2014)
The Glimmering Room (2012)
Ruin (2006)

GUIDEBOOKS FOR THE DEAD

CYNTHIA CRUZ

FOUR WAY BOOKS
TRIBECA

Copyright © 2020 Cynthia Cruz
No part of this book may be used or reproduced in any manner without written permission except in the case of brief quotations embodied in critical articles and reviews.

Library of Congress Cataloging-in-Publication Data

Names: Cruz, Cynthia, author.
Title: Guidebooks for the dead / Cynthia Cruz.
Description: New York : Four Way Books, [2020]
Identifiers: LCCN 2019031740 | ISBN 9781945588440 (trade paperback)
Subjects: LCSH: Dead--Poetry. | Women authors--Poetry. | Creation (Literary, artistic, etc.)--Poetry.
Classification: LCC PS3603.R893 A6 2020 | DDC 811/.6--dc23
LC record available at https://lccn.loc.gov/2019031740

This book is manufactured in the United States of America and printed on acid-free paper.

Four Way Books is a not-for-profit literary press. We are grateful for the assistance we receive from individual donors, public arts agencies, and private foundations.

This publication is made possible with public funds from the National Endowment for the Arts

and from the New York State Council on the Arts, a state agency.

We are a proud member of the Community of Literary Magazines and Presses.

CONTENTS

It is not you who will speak; let the disaster speak in you.

—Maurice Blanchot

ARTAUD

At age five, with his sister Marie-Ange.

Around 1920, at twenty-four.

Around 1920.

At his sister's wedding.

As Cecco, in Marcel Vandal's film *Graziella* (1926).

As Gringalet, in Luitz-Morat's film *Le Juif Errant* (1926).

As Marat, in Abel Gance's *Napoléon* (1926-27).

As Marat.

As the Intellectual, in Léon Poirier's film *Verdun, Visions d'Histoire* (1928).

As the monk Massieu, in Carl Dreyer's *The Passion of Joan of Arc* (1928).

As the father in his play, "The Cenci," produced in 1935 by the Theater of Cruelty.

On the grounds of the asylum in Rodez, with Dr. Fernier in May 1946.

Self-portrait (December 17, 1946).

His room in the clinic in Ivry-sur-Seine.

In his room, shortly before his death.

WEDDING (BERLIN)

The bell of death, my
Little pink mystery.

GUIDEBOOKS FOR THE DEAD

Drink tap water only in large cities.
Drink boiled water and thinned tea.

It is not advisable
Except in hotels.

Take tablets of Resochin Bayer.
Then let it sit

For ten minutes
In potassium permanganate.

Change sweat-soaked underwear.
Wash once a day with soap.

Don't shower more than three times a day
Using one-part mercuric chloride per thousand.

When possible, peel fresh fruit.
When not, wash with soap.

DURAS (POVERTY)

She removes herself from the tremendous stink of poverty.

Poverty. Poverty.

Then, say it again.

Poverty. Detritus, shit.

But, also: glitter, gutter, silver grammar.

From out of the cut comes the sound of the new.

DURAS (SICKNESS)

Alone in the white mansion, M.D. lives, alone. Nothing. No-thing. Just booze and books and old broke vases of long dead roses. She paces. She drinks the cold liquor. When she does, the world is made manifest. Booze, the hinge upon which the world breaks open.

DURAS (THE MUTE)

The poor have no voice. The outsider, the wanderer, the lost and forgotten remain voiceless. Duras's muteness is their voice, is their silence. She holds her voice back—

When we read her words we hear the echo of a scream in her silence. It is the scream of civilization.

DURAS (NOTHINGNESS)

When writing, the writer leaves the world. She vanishes into the folds of her mind. She dies there. Alone, in a field of words. The words are the field, are the words and images of her mind, made manifest, manifold. By writing, the writer leaves her body and enters the page, the text, the otherworld, the one she dreams.

When writing, the writer dies. She dies to the world. The phone, the bloody black ringer, rings on; the birds sing outside the shut glass window, the writer is gone. Writing is transformation, transportation. By writing, the writer leaves. Her body remains. Her body, a terrible hump of flesh and blood, cells and disease. But she is given the gift, grace—she is able to escape her body and the world. She is transported via the electricity inside her mind into the page, into the sea of the words.

M.D. becomes nothing by writing. By thinking, already escapes. Poverty and drinking, destitution, isolation, a lifetime of abandonment. And memory. Booze loosens it up. Booze closes it down. Writing is the same, though different. Writing breaks down all the doors, smashes all the windows in the house, her great big white mansion—and she is free.

UNTITLED

Saint Francis making his way
Into the great desert

With nothing
But his wooden stick.

I am falling behind.

DURAS (THE DEAD)

Duras died in childhood. Poverty, shame. Everything past the age of fifteen is chronicled, written down. Like Louise Bourgeois (another lipstick, hosiery ripped lady), whose work derives from one small window of time (the ten years when her father had an affair with her nanny), Duras's entire oeuvre springs from her gaze back at the wreckage. The wreckage gazes back at her and she becomes the wreckage.

GUIDEBOOKS FOR THE DEAD

The starting point
Was mystical.

I could feel something bright
As it left the body.

What I wouldn't give
To go back—

To my tiny, almost
Russian childhood:

Mother in her crimson gown and stage
Make-up: baby

Blue glitter shadow and her long
Beautiful arms

Changing me into her
Small blonde princess.

When the wheel moves by,
Night is gone.

This life is gone.

There will be no other
Life, other than the sweet

Lavender, sweet
Blossoming dream

Of this one.

DURAS (THE WORD)

M.D. feeds her words into the machinery. She presses herself into the text: sweat, blood, excrement.

It is a vile exercise. It is exquisite, this mysteriousness, this act of brute survival.

One thinks of feeding; of pressing oil-soaked bread into the open mouth of a hungry child.

It is vulgar, it is death. It is the white smear of sex.

Piled up, her words are a tower of filthy bodies.

Hunger, poverty, the deep stain of destitution. A clamor of dark bodies leaning against the grime-stained walls of the city.

She feeds the words into her small blue typing machine. The letters stick. They stick.

She presses her liquor-stained fingers onto the plastic glide of the buttons: "M." "D."

DURAS (THE MYSTIC)

The absence Duras describes is the absence of the Thou, of the lover.

God is the Thou.

THE PORCELAIN ROOM

In the Porcelain Room, everything
Is broken, but terribly beautiful.

Bruises and
Scars,

Faces of make-up and tattoos
Of death masks and stars.

The girls and women enter the room,
Gloved and covered in layers of lace.

Mothers and women
Without any children.

We stand in silence,
Our mouths painted crimson.

We are alone inside this,
What once was monstrous

Silence, but what is now
A cream and white procession.

A silvering, like an endless poem
That goes on forever, each woman's voice

Adding her own jeweled song
To the procession until we are one,

Tethered together by our shared tales of terror
And trauma, bled

Together, a new family
Of voices. Like children singing

In choir, or a small band of girls
Erupting in joy

As they discover
Their own true voice.

IN THE PORCELAIN ROOM

Marguerite Duras is showing me
The scars behind the wall.
The juju within the fold.

What is this music
She asks.

In a headdress of bright
Red flowers and vine

She is still a child.

In her gold
Lamé heels, her pale
Cheeks, smeared
Red.

Porcelain shimmering
Broken and glorious.

Hold my hand, Reader,

Clarice Lispector
Whispers.

We are on the raft
Of dead women.

IN THE PORCELAIN ROOM

We are moving toward the end
Of everything.

We are heading toward
The city.

It is on fire.

We are going to retrieve
The corpse of our dead sister.

Naked,
She is

Sitting near the phone,
Smoking, on the stained
Bare mattress.

Blood and cuts and fever.

She leans toward the camera
And whispers.

IN THE PORCELAIN ROOM

Inside the broken hive
Of glass bells and whispers.

Clarice Lispector
Whispers.

The red and black
Creature is the dearest.

Her hands are lost
Someplace.

They are covering
The gape of her mouth.

GUIDEBOOKS FOR THE DEAD

And the enchantment
Of children's hospitals.

Somewhere there is a god,
I swear.

Someone must be in charge.

What is the word, again,
In Spanish

For *useless*?

GLAMORINE

In time or out of time.

I am their lost star.
Their *never be*.

I'll commit crimes
And live inside
This cocoon-like prism
Of my own mind's making.

Criminal, bewilder.

Arachnaid,
Tiny smiley
Plaything.

GUIDEBOOKS FOR THE DEAD

Set the thick, black cream on the porcelain platters
Along the ice-cold floor
Of the locked hotel bathroom.

Set the needle back down
On the spinning black disc

Of the album titled *Self Portrait*
In Silver Lycra and Crimson
Ballet Stockings.

Inside the broken border
Of this bleak

Frame: a gold,
Miniature theater

Replete with border
Of white death flowers.

Now, let the yellow demons come.
Let the soft spell of quiet darkness.

Let, mesmer and stars.

Filth and accretion: books and magazines
Clothes, shoes, and talismans.

Ephemera to ward the shores
Of memory, back.

DURAS (THE MYSTIC)

God is in the bottle.

The word is made manifest when she drinks the sweet liquor from the bottle.

Magic.

MEDICINE AND MAGAZINES

Glitter of leaves near the gutter
At the Museum of Natural Tragedy.

Succulents, bougainvillea, the toilet
Of our history.

California salve: the plum
Like hum of death's white music.

GUIDEBOOKS FOR THE DEAD

The soft machinery of photographs.

Memories of inherited sorrow, or questions, lost.

A summer of wool and excrement.

Rumors, inside the little black plastic box.

I hear his voice: an animal, a doll

Inside the puppet show.

Shit in a cardboard box.

Nothing,

Just the matter of loss and dislocation.

DURAS (THE FLOCK)

Duras is part of a flock of voices: Duras, Lispector, Cixous, Bachmann. Duras is high priestess. She is also the bottom rung. This is how the flock works: everyone on top, everyone on bottom. All are one in the flock.

These ladies with smeared lipstick and torn hosiery. I find my place among them; I join the end of the queue, this parade of wrong voices. I find my place and I join them.

No shame, we swallow the shame and the shame becomes us. It is part of us now, not something to cut off or be rid of.

Our words are tiny pills or bullets, each one packed with memory, packed with a multitude of meaning.

Our words are free of grammar and syntax. Our pages, filled with holes so that the others may join us. We are dumb as children. Curiosity, the thread that pulls us.

I find my place at the end of the line. And I join them.

DURAS (MYSTIC)

Of Christ, she writes, "Like the love of Christ or of J.S. Bach—the two of them breathtakingly equivalent."

Of the Old Testament, she writes, "The Text of Texts is the Old Testament."

Of God and alcohol she writes: "Alcohol doesn't console, it doesn't fill up anyone's psychological gaps, all it replaces is the lack of God."

M.D.'s sense of the absence of God is common among saints and believers. To notice the lack of God is to sense the place or space He would be. It is to believe, in the first place. This lack is, of course, noticeable only by those who believe. One cannot notice the absence of something they do not anticipate.

The absence of God is the shadow of God.

DURAS (POVERTY)

"The link with poverty is there in the man's hat, too, for money has got to be brought in, got to be brought in somehow," M.D., *The Lover.*

Poverty is in the language, it is in her gaze back. It seeps and oozes into every poverty-stricken word. Each word is used sparingly as if each word were currency.

It is everywhere. It stains everything.

It is everywhere. It flies about. It watches from every corner of the page.

Poverty is not something one leaves behind. A child born into poverty will always feel its presence at the edges of everything. Even right now, you can feel it—it is in my words, these tiny fractured things.

DURAS (THE WORD)

Our origins define us.
We cannot escape our origins.
Like Lispector, Duras's very being is mired in poverty and trauma. She is a stain on a map. She is one of the hungry. This song is the song that sings into all of her soiled music.

Dirty, filthy child.

She creates the world from the word.

By renaming herself, she becomes another. She becomes the character she creates by marking down the words. The author, the writer, subsumed the poor, pale, sick girl from Saigon. This girl, *Duras,* is intellect, is shimmer and brilliance.

"For where the mind is, there is the treasure." Mary Magdalene.

The word, *Duras*, digests her: she becomes the word.

It is an operation, it is painful and gruesome but in the end, she is transformed completely. She is *Duras*.

DURAS (THE WORD)

The word, *Duras*, another word, not hers.
Donnadieu, her surname. *Duras*, the name of her father's village.

She renames herself. Quiet death.

"It's not that you have to achieve anything, it's that you have to get away from where you are."

Duras, Duras. The name becomes her.

WHISKEY, DEATH, OR THE BOOK

Hotel rooms with crystal
Chandeliers and the habit of medicine.
Broken china and the trick
Of vanishing.
A bright, red bead of pomp
And the fever of trauma:
My mother's silver rayon gown
With brother's sky-blue
Pony sneakers. Stars. Alone
In the dark ceremony of the garden:
Painting my face a white mask,
In preparation for another child-like game
Of death.

LITTLE PARISIAN CAKES

Hoarding stacks of lemon tortes
For you.

Small tongues
Of dark chocolates

For the long drive home
Through the shock of forest.

Red, the wool
Skirt and silver, the buckles.

Your sparkling butterfly
Bracelet.

In the end, I hold
Your humming cages.

Your tiny silent
Parade of deaths.

DREAM SALVE

Silver bugs in the glass cupboard.
The dream veil arrives again, my need

To sleep or what
It might take

To break free
From the frame.

What world is this:
Everything broke

And emptied
Of meaning.

GUIDEBOOKS FOR THE DEAD

Walnut bread
Fresh milk, and silver
Tins of German chocolate.

Books in piles and letters
From father
Before he went blind.

Old ripped Greek
Blankets for the two cats.

It isn't much.

But it is
Enough.

GUIDEBOOKS FOR THE DEAD

Or the beginnings of deadly illness.

I exist only inside its murky frame.
Dirt and dregs, filth and silt.

Mother's red and silver suitcase
Filled with old lottery tickets and photographs.

Everything behind us
Is before us

Stretched out: an endless
Grey horizon.

What we don't remember,
Lives in us, forever.

GUIDEBOOKS FOR THE DEAD

Oh bright red lamp, oh flame.

Oh leaked mascara
Caked at the bottom
Of my brown leather satchel.

Alone, my only
Friend: feral, an animal,

And the bright red lamp
That leads me.

GUIDEBOOKS FOR THE DEAD

Now the ghost fears
Have gone.

Just the hemmed-in
The real

Ones. The pill gown
Pitch of death and her shoddy
Song of sorry.

Nothing, just me
Pressed against the oil

Smeared gates
Of the world.

GUIDEBOOKS FOR THE DEAD

Mother's crimson leather bags
Crammed with saint cards
And tiny glass bottles.

The bright stitch
Of God's final coming.

Dirt and dregs,
Silt and stars.

The sweet song
Of poverty

Rinsing through
Like the memory
Of a dream.

GUIDEBOOKS FOR THE DEAD

Blonder, in the pharmacy
I buy magic creams and medicine.

What,
To kill off.

But I cannot stop

Forgetting

A humming like metal in weather.

The terrible black diamond
Of poverty.

DURAS (NOTHINGNESS)

Like Lispector, Cixous, and Bachmann, her strange sisters, Duras's work is filled with holes. The holes are spaces for hesitation, for holding back at the precipice of civilization's giant yawn. What can be said? These women writers understand that to say too much, to babble and garble is to take one's place in the line of acquiescence, to participate in the unwritten *Yes*. Instead, they make a language of silence, leaving holes in their syntax, on the page for *No,* for *But, Yet,* for the stream of unheard voices to join in.

DURAS (NOTHINGNESS)

Nothing is the only appropriate response to civilization. Anything else is mindless babble, simply mirroring the grammar and syntax of gossip and small talk. Duras's makes a new language, a language that is capable of speaking to these atrocities.

". . . there should be non-writing, and it will come some day. A simple language without grammar. A form of writing consisting only of words. Words without grammar to sustain them, abandoned as soon (as) they have been written down."

DURAS (THE MUTE)

"Writing also means not speaking. Keeping silent." M.D., *Writing*.

M.D. is mute. She throws her voice into the text and there, her voice, resides. There, in the book, we hear her screams, we hear her weeping. But alone, in her giant white mansion, she speaks to no one. She paces, endlessly, the only sound, the sound of flies and death emanating from within the cracked walls.

DURAS (ON GOD AND BOOZE)

When the writer is writing she experiences a religious state. What else can do this? Booze can do this. And M.D. was also skilled in the use of booze. Booze, in fact, allowed for this transportation. Booze, the key. Booze, the catalyst, the smeary oil that allowed the windows to break open.

FLÖH

after Tacita Dean

Berlin, the towering
Silver tower

With its blue
Mercedes in the snow.

And its tick
Of tiny gold click.

Time, the lace of dust,
A trace of.

The *fernseher*,
Its dumb white static.

And the small blonde
Dreg of memory

Dragging the drum
Of memory down.

MAGIC

I’m channeling God, again.
I want to be made perfect:
The Warholian magic
Of transformation: Candy Darling
In long blonde wig and crimson
Scarf. What I wouldn’t give
To be a girl, again,
Playing alone with my toy
Wolves in the shut bedroom.
Inside another yellow dream.

THE SIBERIAN WOLF AND HORSE

Poverty and sorrow
Change the face.

Everything I own,
I sold.

Silver liner along the eyes and cobalt
Cream eyeshadow.

Living inside
The desert missile range.

White ash chalk.
Small lace dust

Of what
Is left.

DIARY OF MAGIC

Warburg in the desert
Cataloguing hits of prayer and magic.

Delicate, and the tremendous dream
Of belief seeping out from him.

GUIDEBOOKS FOR THE DEAD

Set the thick, white cream
On the porcelain platter.

Then let the demoning
Angels come.

Let mesmer and stars.

A hum like metal
And the beginnings
Of illness.

GREENPOINT MORNING

The bus begins blocks away.
Its awful heart and then its body
Comes to me.

Past the hotel, an engine
Of men's bodies, then their awful
Grey-white souls,
The liver and spleens.

Drunk, they collapse
On the pavement and let
God love them
All over again.

SELF PORTRAIT IN PORCELAIN TUB

In bright red and orange
V-neck lycra
Swimsuit with glass beads.

I am myself,
Again.

Transfixed
Inside an invisible
Skein of music.

CHARCOAL

In my brown leather bag:
Some underwear and a white feather
I found along the pavement
On Sunset in Silverlake
When I was eleven.
Sweet Marianne playing
On the black plastic radio
In the tremendous muck and doom.
On the train to Versailles:
Three girls from Basque, and the one
Painting her short boy-like nails black.

GUIDEBOOKS FOR THE DEAD

Where is the coat
God gave me:

Long and mink
And to save me.

Under the blue awning
Of the shelter in the rain.

Beneath the shadow
Of the cathedral.

I pull the bell on the string at the gate
Then all the demons came.

ANALOGUE

A photograph and the black
Marks of memory.

Fixed inside the archive
Of the mind

Like a memory.

ON THE TRAIN TO VERSAILLES

Of anesthesia. Of tin bins of names
piled up in numbers.

A Béla Tarr-like winter: an old water-pocked
Calendar discovered among the ruins.

The blacking archive of history,
Finally, all the sweet windows sealed shut.

ON THE TRAIN TO VERSAILLES

Cracked glass of Christ
In its silver vessel,
An ambulatory vitrine.
The relic of my broken
Glass jar of Chanel
Vamp polish, spilled black
Dregs at the bottom
Of my leather bag.

I am leaving, again.

GUIDEBOOKS FOR THE DEAD

When I ask God
He says, Yes

You may vanish.

And just like that
I become

One with the astonishing
Blue envelope of music.

RADIOENTFREMDUNG

My tiny black plastic radio
Is playing death, again.

ACKNOWLEDGMENTS:

Academy of American Poets, *American Poetry Review, Burning House Press, Epiphany, Field, Gulf Coast Online, Guernica, Like Starlings, Moevement, Mud City Review, No Tokens, Plume, Psychology Tomorrow, Riot of Perfume, The Offing, The Literary Hub, The Rumpus, Visceral Brooklyn,* and *West Branch.*

Cynthia Cruz is the author of five previous collections of poetry, including four with Four Way Books: *The Glimmering Room* (2012), *Wunderkammer* (2014), *How the End Begins* (2016), and *Dregs* (2018). Cruz has received various fellowships and has an MFA from Sarah Lawrence College in writing, an MFA in Art Criticism & Writing from the School of Visual Arts, and an MA in German Studies from Rutgers University. The author of a collection of essays, *Disquieting: Essays on Silence* (2019), Cruz is the editor of the anthology, *Other Musics: New Latina Poetry* (2019). She teaches at Columbia University and Sarah Lawrence College.

Publication of this book was made possible by grants and donations. We are also grateful to those individuals who participated in our 2019 Build a Book Program. They are:

Anonymous (14), Sally Ball, Vincent Bell, Jan Bender-Zanoni, Laurel Blossom, Adam Bohannon, Lee Briccetti, Jane Martha Brox, Anthony Cappo, Carla & Steven Carlson, Andrea Cohen, Janet S. Crossen, Marjorie Deninger, Patrick Donnelly, Charles Douthat, Morgan Driscoll, Lynn Emanuel, Blas Falconer, Monica Ferrell, Joan Fishbein, Jennifer Franklin, Sarah Freligh, Helen Fremont & Donna Thagard, Ryan George, Panio Gianopoulos, Lauri Grossman, Julia Guez, Naomi Guttman & Jonathan Mead, Steven Haas, Bill & Cam Hardy, Lori Hauser, Bill Holgate, Deming Holleran, Piotr Holysz, Nathaniel Hutner, Elizabeth Jackson, Rebecca Kaiser Gibson, Dorothy Tapper Goldman, Voki Kalfayan, David Lee, Howard Levy, Owen Lewis, Jennifer Litt, Sara London & Dean Albarelli, David Long, Ralph & Mary Ann Lowen, Jacquelyn Malone, Fred Marchant, Donna Masini, Louise Mathias, Catherine McArthur, Nathan McClain, Richard McCormick, Kamilah Aisha Moon, James Moore, Beth Morris, John Murillo & Nicole Sealey, Kimberly Nunes, Rebecca Okrent, Jill Pearlman, Marcia & Chris Pelletiere, Maya Pindyck, Megan Pinto, Barbara Preminger, Kevin Prufer, Martha Rhodes, Paula Rhodes, Silvia Rosales, Linda Safyan, Peter & Jill Schireson, Jason Schneiderman, Roni & Richard Schotter, Jane Scovell, Andrew Seligsohn & Martina Anderson, Soraya Shalforoosh, Julie A. Sheehan, James Snyder & Krista Fragos, Alice St. Claire-Long, Megan Staffel, Marjorie & Lew Tesser, Boris Thomas, Pauline Uchmanowicz, Connie Voisine, Martha Webster & Robert Fuentes, Calvin Wei, Bill Wenthe, Allison Benis White, Michelle Whittaker, Rachel Wolff, and Anton Yakovlev.